T is for Taj Mahal

An India Alphabet

Written by Varsha Bajaj and Illustrated by Robert Crawford

For my parents
Shashi and Nima Walavalkar

VARSHA

❧

To my two wonderful children: my daughter Katie, who loves to
travel and is always an inspiration, and Jamie, whose artwork I have
great admiration for. With this book, I strive to inspire them.

ROBERT

Text Copyright © 2011 Varsha Bajaj
Illustration Copyright © 2011 Robert Crawford

Sleeping Bear Press®
315 E. Eisenhower Parkway, Suite 200
Ann Arbor MI 48108
www.sleepingbearpress.com

Sleeping Bear Press is an imprint of Gale, a part of Cengage Learning.

10 9 8 7 6 5 4 3 2 1

Printed by China Translation & Printing Services Limited, Guangdong Province, China.
1st printing.   11/2010

Library of Congress Cataloging-in-Publication Data

Bajaj, Varsha.
T is for Taj Mahal : an India alphabet / written by Varsha Bajaj ; illustrated
by Robert Crawford.
p. cm.
Includes bibliographical references and index.
ISBN 978-1-58536-504-3 (alk. paper)
1. India—Juvenile literature. 2. English language—Alphabet—Juvenile
literature. 3. Alphabet books. I. Crawford, Robert, 1953- ill. II. Title.
 DS407.B318 2011
  954—dc22   2010030500

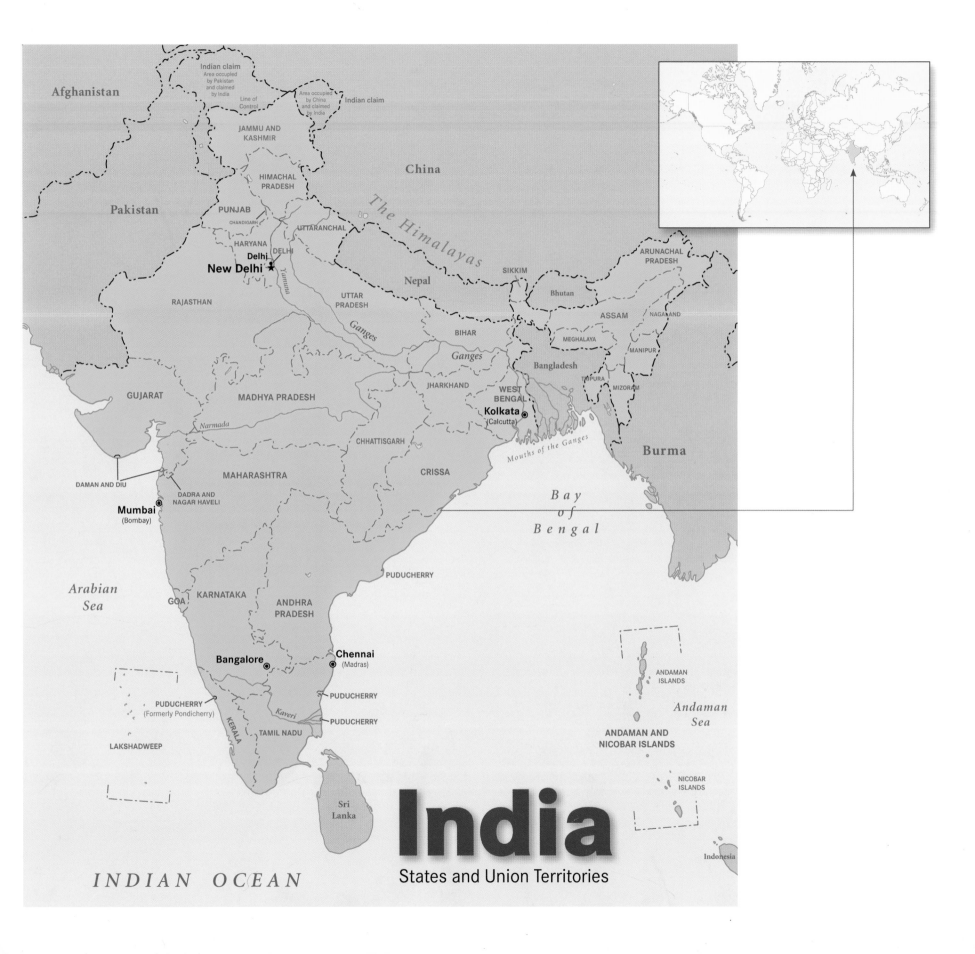

India

States and Union Territories

Aa

The history of the Aryan people in India is told in the Hindu sacred text or scriptures called the Vedas (1500–1200 BC). *Veda* means knowledge. The Aryans came from Central Asia and were considered hardy, tough people, fierce and warlike. In the ancient Sanskrit language *Aryas* meant "noble."

Before the Aryans, the Dravidians were India's main cultural and ethnic group. The Aryans began to invade and rule over the northern parts of India, pushing the Dravidian people south. Over centuries, Aryan society grew into a system of social ranks (or castes) that still influences Indian society today.

But, there was civilization in the valley of the Indus River dating even further back to 2600 BC. Archaeologists discovered the buried ruins of two huge cities, Harappa and Mohenjo-daro, in the 1920s. The archaeologists were amazed to discover that the ancient Indus people were as advanced as the ancient Egyptians and flourished about the same time as the ancient Greek civilizations. They built cities with efficient drainage systems and their houses were as high as three stories.

A is for Aryans

Ancient history tells us
the Aryans came to stay.
The Vedas tell us stories
about life in their day.

B is for Bollywood

Movies for the masses,
full of song and dance,
handsome heroes and villains,
pretty girls to romance.

The Hindi-language cinema industry based in Mumbai is called Bollywood, a word that combines the words Bombay and Hollywood. The city of Mumbai was called Bombay until 1997. Some people don't like the word Bollywood because it makes the industry seem secondary to Hollywood, California. But Bollywood represents an important and thriving Indian film industry.

India also has thriving regional cinema centers producing films in other Indian languages: Bengali, Tamil, and Marathi. India produces the largest number of films in the world, approximately 700 a year in all the languages.

A typical Bollywood film, meant to entertain the entire family, includes song and dance, drama, comedy, and action. Bollywood stars are huge celebrities with millions of fans. A film's soundtrack is a crucial part of the production and is released to fans before the movie to create anticipation and excitement.

Bollywood movie dialogue is spoken in Hindi but includes subtitles in many languages such as English, Spanish, and French, so that audiences that don't understand Hindi can enjoy them. Bollywood films are seen all over south Asia, Russia, and wherever an immigrant Indian population is found: America, Great Britain, the Middle East, and parts of Africa.

Bb

India loves cricket and its cricket players, called cricketers. Cricket is a team sport played with a bat and ball. The bat is made of wood and is shaped like a flat blade topped with a handle. The ball has a hard core with a leather outer covering. Batsmen have to wear helmets and pads to protect themselves from being hit by the fast-flying ball.

In cricket, each team has 11 players. One team bats, trying to score as many runs as possible by running back and forth the length of the field without being struck out. The other team pitches and fields to strike out the first team's batsmen and limit any runs being scored. Then it's the other team's turn at bat. At its simplest there are similarities to baseball, but the scoring, and cricket's many rules are quite different. For example, cricket games can last for several days!

Though cricket is the favorite game, it is not India's national sport. The national sport is field hockey, and India has national men's and women's field hockey teams. From 1928 to 1956 the Indian men's team won six consecutive field hockey Olympic gold medals.

C is for Cricket

Cricket is a passion—
a game with bat and ball.
Introduced by the British
it's embraced by one and all

D d

Lush fabrics from India
have stood the test of time.
The elegant *sari*,
forever in its prime.

The *sari* (SAH-ree), worn by Indian women, has been around for hundreds of years. It is unstitched fabric, typically 6 meters (almost 20 feet) in length. It is wrapped around the waist with one end draped over the left shoulder. The midriff area is bared. The sari is worn over a skirt and a cropped, fitted blouse. The sari can be cotton for daily wear or woven from silks, chiffons, and brocades for formal occasions. The fabrics are of vivid colors and may be embellished with gold embroidery, mirrors, or sequins. If you go to India you will see the *sari*, the *salwar kameez* and also Western clothes. The *salwar kameez* (sul-vaar-kha-MEEZ) is also worn by women and originated in northern India. It consists of loose drawstring pants with a knee-length tunic and a scarf, or *dupatta*, over it.

Traditional attire for men is the *dhotis* (duh-HO-tee) which is a long piece of fabric wrapped around the legs and waist. The *sherwanis* (sher-VA-nee) which is a long jacket is more formal. The Nehru jacket, made popular by India's first prime minister, Jawaharlal Nehru, is shorter than a traditional sherwani.

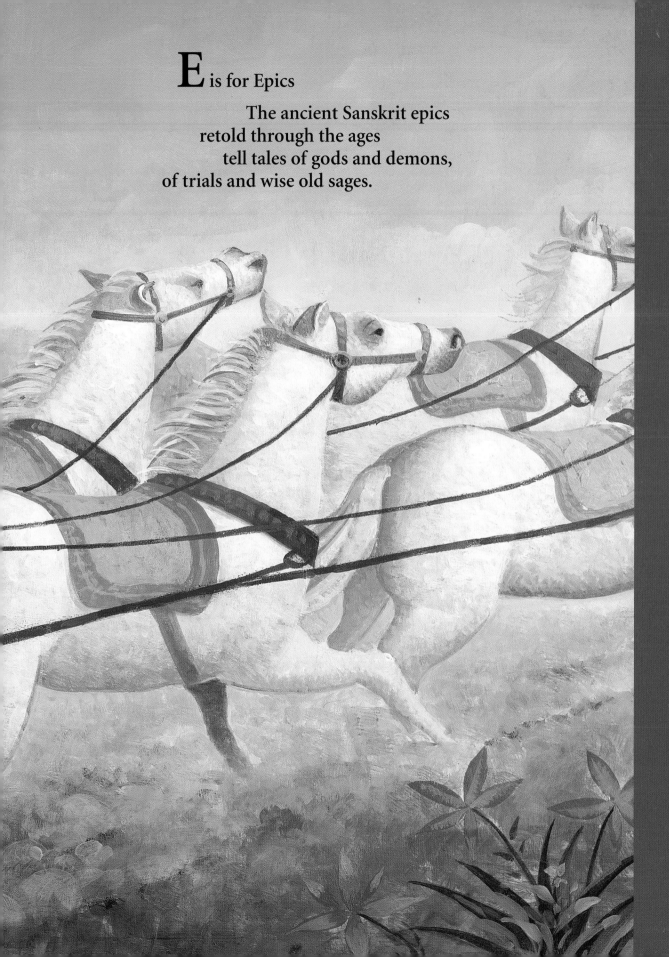

E is for Epics

The ancient Sanskrit epics
retold through the ages
tell tales of gods and demons,
of trials and wise old sages.

Indian mythology is filled with epic stories about gods (*devas*) and demons (*asuras*). The two main epics, the Ramayana and the Mahabharata, are told in Sanskrit, the classical language of India. These were written in ancient times.

The epic poem, The Ramayana, is approximately 50,000 lines long and was written by India's celebrated poet Valmiki about the life of Lord Rama. It is the story of Rama's journey from his birth to his exile, his fight to save his wife from the demon Ravana, his victory over evil, and his homecoming.

The second epic, the Mahabharata, was written by the poet Vyasa and is the longest poem in the world. The Bhagavad Gita, one of Hinduism's sacred texts, is part of this book. It is a dialogue on the eve of war in which the Hindu god Krishna teaches the archer Arjuna the lessons of life and the importance of doing one's duty, no matter how painful.

The main message of the epics is that of good conduct, or *dharma*, fearlessness, dedication and duty, and the victory of good over evil.

F is for Festivals

Autumn brings Diwali—
the Festival of Lights.
Holi celebrates the spring
with colors sprinkled bright.

Diwali is the most important festival in four religions—Hinduism, Sikhism, Buddhism, and Jainism—practiced in India. Diwali, in Sanskrit, means "a row of lights." Small clay oil lamps are lit to signify the victory of good over evil.

The five-day festival occurs on the new moon between mid-October and mid-November, according to the Hindu lunar calendar. Diwali is the celebration of the homecoming of the Hindu god Ram and his wife, Seeta, after fourteen years of exile, and his victory over the evil king Ravana.

During Diwali, children and adults wear new clothes and receive gifts. Schools and offices are closed. Many kinds of sweets and snacks are made and enjoyed by family and friends. Fireworks are a part of the celebration. Homes are decorated and cleaned, and it is believed that during Diwali Lakshmi, the goddess of wealth, visits the house and blesses it.

Holi is celebrated to welcome spring. People toss colored powders and water on each other and Lord Krishna is remembered. Children especially love this messy and fun festival.

Ff

Mohandas Gandhi (1869–1948) was India's foremost spiritual and political leader. In India he is affectionately called *bapu*, which means "father." His birthday, October 2, is a national holiday in India and is celebrated worldwide as the International Day of Non-Violence.

Gandhi believed in:
- Civil disobedience, which is the active but peaceful refusal to obey certain laws made by the government—in this case the ruling British in 1930s India.
- Non-violence, *ahimsa*, (a-him-sa). Ghandi said, "An eye for an eye makes the whole world blind."
- Peaceful resistance, *satyagraha*, (SUHT-yuh-gruh-huh).

Gandhi led a very simple life in a self-supporting residential community (an *ashram*) and only wore clothes made from yarn that he spun himself. He also was a vegetarian. Gandhi fought for social reform, women's rights, and for the rights of the downtrodden.

Gandhi was assassinated on January 30, 1948, by a man who believed that Gandhi had weakened the country during its partition into India and Pakistan in 1947.

G is for Gandhi

He was called Mahatma, Sanskrit for "great soul." India free from British rule was his primary goal.

Himalayas, in Sanskrit, means the abode or home of snow. *Hima* is snow and *alaya* means home. The Himalayan range stretches across six countries: Afghanistan, Bhutan, China, India, Nepal, and Pakistan. The highest mountain peak in the world, Mount Everest, in Nepal, stands 29,029 feet tall. The highest peak in India is part of the Kanchenjunga mountain at 28,208 feet. Its name means "five treasures of snow" referring to its five peaks.

The snow from the Himalayas melts into nineteen major rivers including the Indus, Ganges, and Brahmaputra rivers that flow across the plains of India. The Himalayas have shaped the cultures of south Asia, and many Himalayan peaks are sacred in both Hinduism and Buddhism. These mountains formerly served as a natural defense for India, securing it against invasion from the north.

H h

H is for Himalayas

The mighty Himalayas
are the giants of the north.
The world's great adventurers
their majestic peaks call forth.

I is for Independent India

Independence was won
after a long, hard fight.
In 1947
India strode into the light.

The British began trading goods in India in the early 1700s. Seen as a vast potential of wealth because of its spices, India was fought over by the English, the French, and others. Initially the British were only interested in India as a trading partner, but things changed over time and they began to see India as a colony. In 1876 Queen Victoria was proclaimed Empress of India.

The British drained India of its wealth and resources, but they also built the railroad system and set up a centralized government and judicial system. Led by Gandhi and Nehru, India united politically against the British. At the stroke of midnight on August 15, 1947, India became a free country, and at that time the country was partitioned into the Republic of India in the south and the Islamic Republic of Pakistan in the north. Millions were displaced in this violent separation. India's constitution came into effect in 1950 and declared that all Indians, regardless of caste, religion, or creed were equal citizens of the new republic. In 1952 India held its first general election and became the world's largest democracy—a distinction India still holds today.

Ii

J is for Jewelry

Ruby, pearl, and emerald—
gems inlaid in gold;
a bejeweled Indian bride
is a wondrous sight to behold.

The various regions of India have diverse styles and designs of jewelry. The kings and queens of old adorned their feet, hands, necks, and fingers with jewels. In the past, a woman's jewels were the only wealth she could own. They were also her only form of security and therefore extremely precious to her. Jewels were given to a woman as a dowry at the time of her marriage. While times and traditions have changed, many Indians remain fascinated with jewelry and gold today.

Jewelry also has symbolic value. For example, diamonds signify Venus, coral signifies Mars, blue sapphire signifies Saturn, yellow sapphire represents Jupiter, and emerald signifies Mercury. Rubies signify the sun, and pearls the moon. Two other symbolic gems are hessonite and cat's eye. The nine stones together are called *Nav-ratna* and are worn to promote good health and keep away bad luck.

The Mughals (Islamic rulers of India) influenced Indian jewelry with *kundan*, or setting of gems in strips of gold, and *meenakari*, enameling. In most parts of India, a bride on her wedding day wears a red sari and a lot of jewels and gold.

J j

K k

Beautiful swirling costumes,
bells on dancers' feet,
dancing from the ages;
watching is a treat.

Kathak is a north Indian classical dance form. There are different forms of Indian classical dance and each has its own style, costume, and roots. The two oldest classical temple dance forms are Bharatnatyam, which originated in southern India, and Odissi, which has its roots in eastern India. All the forms tell stories from the myths. The expression of emotions and the evocation of the divine are very important elements in classical dance. The dancers wear elaborate, colorful, beautiful costumes usually made from silk and other rich fabrics. They wear beautiful traditional jewelry. They have bells on their feet that make music of their own along with the beat of the dancing music. Many of these performances can be seen as dance drama, like ballets, where stories are told through dance. There are several other folk dance forms such as the Bhangra from northern India and Garba from the Indian state of Gujrat.

Dances are key to Bollywood films, where they draw inspiration both from the classical Indian forms and Western forms such as hip-hop, ballet, and jazz dance.

Languages in India have two main origins. Dravidian languages are spoken in the southern states and Indo-Aryan languages are spoken in the northern states. In British India, English was the only language used for administrative and higher-education purposes. After independence, in 1950, Hindi and English were both declared official languages, and each state was given the freedom to choose the official language of the state. Thus non-Hindi speaking Indians would not have difficulty in communicating.

Each state, however, has the power to choose an official language for itself. India thus has 22 official languages today. Marathi, Tamil, Punjabi, and Malayalam are some of them.

Would you like to learn some Hindi words? To greet someone in Hindi you would say *namaste* (na-MA-stay). *Shukriya* (Shook-REE-yah) means thank you.

"How are you?" is *Aap kaise ho*? (Aap ka-say ho?). Many Indian words have found their way into the English language. Bungalow, pajama, and karma are all words of Indian origin.

L

L is for Languages

India's many languages
reflect its society—
Hindi, Tamil, Marathi,
full of variety.

bungalow

jungle

yoga

cheetah

pajama

The music of India ranges from folk music to music from Indian films, to classical music. Each region also has its own folk music. Popular music is typically from films. Music is also a part of all celebrations and worship.

Hindustani and Carnatic music are the two classical forms of music. Hindustani music developed primarily in northern India and has Persian and Mughal influences. Its roots date back to Vedic times but it was developed around the thirteenth and fourteenth centuries AD. Carnatic music developed in southern India and dates back to the fifteenth and sixteenth centuries. In classical Indian music, compositions are based on a *raga* or a set of notes that depicts moods, seasons, or times of the day.

Ravi Shankar and the sitar were responsible for introducing northern Indian classical music to the world. A sitar is an Indian stringed instrument with a long, hollow neck. In the 1960s Ravi Shankar's collaboration with George Harrison, a member of the rock group The Beatles, from England, became very popular in the United States and helped to make Indian classical music popular in the West.

M
m

M is for Music

Music is a part
of India's cultural beat,
from folk songs to the sitar,
that echo on every street.

South Asia consists of Bangladesh, Bhutan, India, the Maldives, Nepal, Pakistan, and Sri Lanka. Some definitions may also include Afghanistan, Myanmar, and Tibet. Many of these countries were once British colonies and part of the old silk and spice route to Europe and the Middle East.

South Asia is home to places of immense natural beauty and holds more than one-fifth of the world's population, making it both the most populous and most densely populated geographical region in the world.

India's population is 120 billion. Since the mid-1950s the government has tried to educate India's people about the benefits of limiting family size.

The region has often seen conflicts and political instability, including wars between the region's neighbors Pakistan and India, both of which have nuclear weapons. Both countries hope for peaceful coexistence, given their shared history and culture.

N is for Neighbors

The South Asian region:
  Maldives, India, Nepal.
Home to several billions
  in countries large and small.

India is surrounded by the Indian Ocean and the Arabian Sea and has several mighty rivers. The Indian Ocean is the third-largest ocean in the world, holding 20 percent of the earth's salt water. The Indian Ocean provides major sea routes connecting the Middle East, Africa, and East Asia with Europe and the Americas and carrying petroleum from the oil fields of the Persian Gulf and Indonesia.

The river Ganga, or the Ganges, personified in Hinduism as a goddess, Mother Ganga, is sacred to Indians. It is believed that taking a dip in the river will wash away one's sins. The Ganges Action Plan was initiated by the government in 1985 to clean up the river. Devout Hindus make pilgrimages to bathe in the Ganga and to meditate on its banks.

Yamuna, Narmada, and Kaveri are the other major rivers that have a place in Hindu mythology. Kaveri is considered the Ganga of the south.

O is for Ocean

The vast Arabian Sea,
the sparkling Indian Ocean,
the flowing sacred Ganges
are poetry in motion.

P p

In America the president is the leader of the country but in India the prime minister is the head of the government. India follows a parliamentary system modeled on Great Britain's. The prime minister is the leader of the majority party in the Lok Sabha.

There are two houses of the Parliament in India called the *Lok Sabha* (people's assembly) and the *Rajya Sabha* (council of states). The prime minister is elected for a period of five years; at the end of five years elections are held. Two members of the Lok Sabha's 545 members and twelve members of the Rajya Sabha's 543 members are appointed by the president; the rest are elected.

Jawaharlal Nehru was India's first prime minister. He took office in August 1947 and was prime minister until his death in May 1964.

India has had the distinction of having had a woman prime minister. Indira Gandhi was Nehru's daughter and was prime minister from January 1966 to March 1977. She was reelected in January 1980 and governed until her assassination on October 31, 1984.

P is for Prime Minister

The leader of the country
with the power to command.
Nehru, Shastri, Indira
have ruled in this great land.

Qutab Minar is the tallest brick minaret in the world at 728 feet. There are 379 stairs inside the tower, which lead to the top. It is listed by the United Nations World Heritage Site as a place of special cultural or physical significance deemed to be of "outstanding universal value."

The foundation of the tower was laid by Qutubu'd–Din Aibak, the first Mughal ruler of India, in 1199 AD, and the first floor was completed during his reign. The entire structure was finished in 1386. In the past the call for prayer would be issued from the top of the Minar.

The Qutab Minar is made up of red and buff sandstone and covered with intricate carvings and verses from the Holy Qur'an. According to legend, anyone who can encircle the entire nearby Iron Pillar with his or her arms, with their back toward the pillar, can have a wish granted.

Q q

Q is for Qutab Minar

The world's tallest minaret
built from red brick,
    a symbol of Islamic design,
completed in 1386.

Rr

R is for Religion

Hinduism and Buddhism
were born in this land.
Tolerance of all faiths
is a constitutional command.

India, known as the land of spirituality, was the birthplace of Hinduism, Buddhism, Jainism, and Sikhism. Eighty percent of Indians in India are Hindu, which means they believe in karma—the sum total of a person's good and bad deeds.

Islam is the second-largest religious group in India and is based on the belief in one god and follows the teachings of the prophet Muhammad.

Christians, believers in the teachings of Jesus Christ, are the third-largest religious group in India with approximately 24 million followers.

Jains believe that the universe and everything in it is eternal and are vegetarians who follow a disciplined and peaceful life. Sikhism originated in northern India in the sixteenth century. The current prime minister of India, Manmohan Singh, is a Sikh.

The Constitution of India declares the nation to be a secular country, which means that all citizens have the right to worship freely and practice any religion or faith.

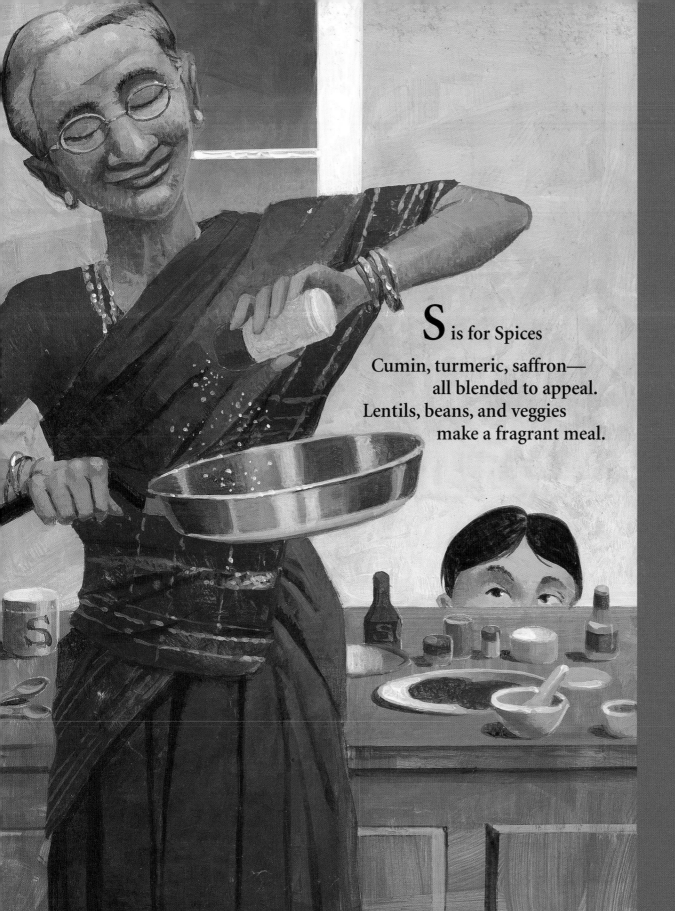

S is for Spices

Cumin, turmeric, saffron—
all blended to appeal.
Lentils, beans, and veggies
make a fragrant meal.

Spices, lentils, beans, and vegetables are the mainstay of Indian food. Frequently used spices are chili pepper, black mustard seed, cumin, turmeric, ginger, coriander, and garlic. A popular spice mix is *garam masala* (ga-rum ma-SAH-la) which is a combination of five or more dried spices, commonly including cardamom, cinnamon, and clove.

Indian cooking is often thought of as "curry." Curry comes from the Tamil word *kari* ("sauce"). A large majority of Indians are vegetarians. Most Hindus don't eat beef and Muslims don't eat pork. The mango is indigenous to the Indian subcontinent and is its national fruit. Dried mango powder or *amchur* (AHM-choor) is a spice commonly used in northern Indian cuisine.

Would you like to make an Indian dessert? You can make *burfi*/milk fudge.

- 15 oz. whole milk ricotta cheese
- 1 stick unsalted butter
- 1 ½ cups sugar
- 1¾ cups dry powdered milk
- ½ tsp. nutmeg or cinnamon
- ¼ cup slivered almonds or chopped unsalted pistachios for garnish

Method: Over low heat, melt the stick of butter in a heavy saucepan. Add the ricotta cheese and sugar to the butter and mix them together. Cook over low heat 5–7 minutes. The mixture is done when bubbles start to form. Be careful— at this point the mixture will be very hot! Turn the heat down to low. Gently stir in the dry milk crystals. Do not try to smooth the crystals out in the mixture, as you want a granular texture. Transfer the mixture into a greased 8x8 dish, cool in the refrigerator for about an hour, cut into squares, and enjoy!

Known as the eighth wonder of the world, the Taj Mahal is located in Agra. In 1631 Mughal Emperor Shah Jahan was grief-stricken when his favorite wife, Mumtaz Mahal, died during the birth of their fourteenth child. (It was customary in those days for the king to have several wives.) In her dying breath she asked him to build a mausoleum for her, one more beautiful than any the world had seen before. Construction of the Taj Mahal began in 1632, one year after her death and was completed in 1653 through the efforts of artisans and craftsmen. The Taj is built of white marble and has forty-three varieties of precious and semiprecious stones inlaid in the marble. It is known for its perfect symmetry. Passages from the Qur'an are engraved on its walls and are used as decorative elements.

Its beauty is particularly striking at dawn and at sunset, and it seems to glow in the light of the full moon.

The Taj Mahal is an example of Mughal architecture, a style that combines Persian, Indian, and Islamic architectural styles. In 1983 the Taj Mahal became a United Nations World Heritage Site.

T is for Taj Mahal

The "Taj" is a monument
to the king's beloved queen.
Its marbled majesty and splendor
is a sight to be seen.

U is for Urban Centers

Calcutta, Mumbai, and Delhi,
bustling, vibrant, alive,
growing, colorful, and noisy,
where millions of Indians thrive.

Approximately 25 percent of India's population lives in its cities. Many Indian cities have been renamed in the past twenty years. For example, Bombay was renamed Mumbai in 1995 and Calcutta was renamed Kolkata in 2001. These changes were a part of moving away from India's British-influenced colonial past and were intended to encourage pride in regional languages and culture.

Mumbai is the financial capital of India, home to the Reserve Bank of India and the National Stock Exchange. The most populous city in India, Mumbai, is the second-most populated in the world, with 14 million people. People from all over India relocate to Mumbai every day in the hope of finding jobs.

New Delhi has been the capital of the country since India became independent in 1947 and is the second-most populated Indian city. It is home to both houses of parliament. It has a long and rich history and has several buildings of interest such as the Red Fort and India Gate.

Bangalore—now Bengaluru—is known as the technology capital of India. It is the nation's leading information technology employer and exporter and is India's fastest-growing city. Kolkata is a vibrant eastern Indian city known for its art and literature.

Uu

V
v

A majority of Indians—about 75 percent—live in rural India. Life in the villages is largely dependent on farming. Because India had experienced famine and hunger in the past, in 1965 the government focused on India becoming self-reliant in its food production. It introduced varieties of high-yield seeds and used better fertilizers and irrigation methods, all designed to make India self-sufficient and to improve life in India's villages.

The difference in the standard of living between India's cities and its rural areas is decreasing, but a lot more has to be done to bring electricity, education, and other services to remote villages. Children living in villages used to work in the fields rather than go to school, but today many receive elementary education provided by the government. More than one-third of all rural households now have a main source of livelihood other than farming.

India's national tree, the Banyan tree or the Indian fig tree, is the focal point of village life and the village council meets under the shade of this tree. The Buddha is believed to have gained enlightenment while meditating under a Banyan tree.

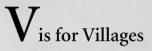

V is for Villages

The rhythm of rural life
revolves around the field.
Cultivating, growing,
praying for bountiful yields.

W is for Wildlife

Peacocks, elephants, and cobras,
monkeys, leopards, and deer
roam the Indian jungles,
where the tiger evokes fear.

India's climate is varied, ranging from the tropical to the arctic. Tigers, snow leopards, antelope, deer, bear, jackals, and hyenas can all be found in India. Several animal and bird sanctuaries exist to preserve this array of wildlife. The Asiatic lion is found in the Gir National Park in western India and the Sunderban National Park in eastern India is home to the Royal Bengal tiger, India's national animal. Many species of deer and wild elephant herds can also be seen. India's national bird, the peacock, is well known for its gorgeous fan of tail feathers.

India's wilderness areas are called jungles, from the Hindi word *jangal*. The term was adopted by the British and has long been part of the English language. Many stories have been set in the jungles of India, including Rudyard Kipling's *The Jungle Book* and the native Jataka tales.

Some animals, such as snakes, monkeys, elephants, and mice are part of Indian mythology. Hindus consider cows to be sacred because they are gentle animals that nurture us like a mother by giving us milk. Buddhists regard the snake as sacred because of the story of Mucalinda, the king cobra who protected the Lord Buddha from the elements as he meditated in search of enlightenment.

Export means legally sending goods to another country for the purpose of selling to, or trading with, that country. In ancient times India exported spices to other parts of the world. India was also famous for its textiles which were a chief item for export in the sixteenth century.

India's main exports to the United States are zinc, sugar, and steel-making materials. India also exports cotton, textiles, chemicals, leather, equipment used in engineering, plastics, gems, and jewelry. India also exports its goods to other developed countries such as the United Kingdom, Belgium, China, Russia, and others.

In the past two decades India has become known for its educated, English-speaking, and hard-working workforce. Many Western countries have outsourced computer-related jobs and other high-technology jobs to India.

The trade partnership between India and the United States is growing quickly. India imports civilian and military aircraft, fertilizers, and telecommunications equipment from the United States.

X x

X is for eXports

From spices to technology,
India's exports aim high.
Selling goods to other countries
where millions are eager to buy.

Yy

Yoga is a physical and spiritual practice aimed at joining the mind, the body, and the spirit. What most people regard as yoga is hatha yoga, which is primarily the practice of the various poses (*asanas*) and breathing (*pranayam*). The lotus pose is named for the lotus flower—India's national flower and a symbol of purity of the heart and mind.

Yoga originated more than 5,000 years ago. The early writings describing the practice of yoga were put on fragile palm leaves instead of paper and were easily damaged; many were lost.

Yoga poses were inspired by nature (mountain and tree poses), by animals (downward-facing dog, cobra), by humans (child pose, warrior pose), and objects (plank pose, bridge pose).

Would you like to learn the tree pose?
- Stand with feet apart. Relax shoulders and let hands hang by sides.
- Exhale, then place left foot on the inside of right thigh, with the toes pointing downward.
- Inhale, then stretch arms sideways to form a T, palms facing down.
- Exhale, and bring palms together in prayer position, fingertips pointing up.

Raise your arms overhead, keeping your palms together. To maintain balance, it helps to focus your eyes on a point in front of you and keep on breathing using your belly. Practicing the tree pose will help improve your balance and concentration.

Y is for Yoga

Yoga is the union
of the body and the mind.
The practice of the poses
bestows peace upon humankind.

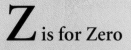

Z is for Zero

India's gift to math
is the invention of the zero.
In seventh century BC
the scholar was a hero.

Have you heard of zero the hero? In today's world we cannot imagine not having the zero. But there was a time when people did not fully understand the concept of zero.

The Babylonians and the Olmecs (present-day Mexico) used zero as a placeholder. What is a placeholder? As an example the zero helps us understand that the number 505 is different from 55.

But it was in India that astronomers and mathematicians came upon the idea of using zero as a number besides being a placeholder.

The rules governing the use of zero appeared for the first time in Brahmagupta's book *Brahmasputha Siddhanta (The Opening of the Universe)*, written in 628 AD. Here Brahmagupta considers not only zero, but negative numbers, and the algebraic rules for the elementary operations of arithmetic with such numbers.

Here are some of the rules of Brahmagupta:
• The sum of zero and a negative number is negative.
• The sum of zero and a positive number is positive.
• The sum of zero and zero is zero.

Z z

Varsha Bajaj

Author Varsha Bajaj was born in Mumbai, India, and lived in a house surrounded by coconut, guava, and beetle nut trees. She came to the United States in 1986 as a graduate student studying psychology. Her first book, *How Many Kisses Do You Want Tonight?* was published by Little, Brown Books for Young Readers in 2004 and was named to the 2005 Texas Library Association 2X2 Reading List. Varsha lives in Houston, Texas with her family. You can find out more about her at www.varshabajaj.com.

Robert Crawford

Robert Crawford's paintings have appeared on the covers of magazines such as *Fortune, Business Week,* and *The Atlantic* and as cover art for best-selling books published by Random House, Penguin/Putnam, Avon, and other major publishers.

His paintings have been included in group shows in New York, Japan, and Germany. Robert recently painted a 50-foot mural for Bank of America that celebrates Chicago's various communities.

His fine art pieces continue to be popular with collectors. Robert works from his studio in northwest Connecticut.